Nike and Phil Knight
How They Grew and Changed the Fashion and Athletic Worlds Forever

Table of Contents

Introduction 4

Chapter 1 – Phil Knight's Background 6

Discovering His Interest In Shoes 7

Knight's Great Partner 9

Chapter 2 – Growing Nike 11

Opening Retail Stores 12

The Split 14

A New Vision 15

Creating Good Shoe Principles 16

Introducing the Cortez 17

The First Endorsement 18

Chapter 3 – Changing Products and Growing 20

Creating New Shoes 21

Watching Endorsements 22

Chapter 4 – Simple Struggles and How They Were Fixed 24

Endorsement Charges 24

Trying To Reach Women 25

The Struggle With Creativity 27

Chapter 5 – The Air Jordan 28

An Extended Relationship 30

Chapter 6 – Moving Forward 32

The Nike Air Max **32**

A Special Slogan **33**

Keep an Ethical Image **34**

Expanding Its Reach **36**

Chapter 7 – Recent Developments **37**

His Work Outside Nike **39**

The End **40**

Conclusion – What You Can Learn From Phil Knight **41**

Unique Ideas **41**

Effort **42**

A Drive To Move Forward **42**

Introduction

The odds are you've seen some high-quality Nike shoes or athletic apparel at some point today. Whether it's from someone on the street, someone at a gym or an athlete on television, you might be surprised at how ubiquitous Nike has become. Indeed, Nike has become a very popular name in the world of athletic shoes. Today people sport a variety of Nike shoes for running and basketball use all around the world. Nike has also become a big name in the field of athletic wear.

In fact, Nike continues to be a true trend setter when it comes to shoes. Whenever Nike introduces a new shoe model promoted by a highly popular athlete, people will line up outside stores to be the first to get these shoes.

The amazing thing about Nike is that it is a brand that grew out of the trunk of one man's car. Nike had not always been a big name in the world of shoes. It started out rather small out in Oregon as Phil Knight wanted to find ways to make new shoes and to sell them to people.

Over the years Phil Knight has become a powerful name in the world of shoes. His amazing ideas and plans for success helped him to succeed as he started to sell his shoes to more people.

The story of Phil Knight has especially become important as it shows how important effort can be. This includes not only working hard to make products more visible but also to create new products with ideas that were unique and different from what people might have found in different places.

As you will read here, Nike has certainly grown over the years to include a variety of great products. However, the effort that Knight used to get Nike to grow is what truly helped get Nike to succeed to where it is today.

The work that Phil Knight has performed over the years came out of a simple exploration that he had with regards to how well shoes could work. This includes a good look at how well shoes can be made and how he could sell them.

This book also delves into a look at how well Knight grew Nike with the help of many people. From his old track and field coach to many legendary athletes, he received plenty of support to help him carry through with his plans and to keep growing and thriving.

You will certainly be inspired when you discover just what got Nike to become a popular name in the world of shoes. It's a great brand name that has become internationally famous – and it all started off of a simple idea and in the back of a car.

Chapter 1 – Phil Knight's Background

To understand how Phil Knight became a big name in the world of shoes, it helps to understand what got him to this spot. He has been in the field for more than fifty years. But it is amazing as to how different things had been well in the past.

Phil Knight was born in 1938 in Portland, Oregon. He got into running at an early age and even got some of his earliest experience when he worked for the Oregonian, a newspaper in the area. He ran to and from his job every day.

He attended the University of Oregon in Eugene and graduated in 1959 with a journalism degree. While at Oregon, he was a track athlete who once ran a mile in four minutes and ten seconds. He also won three varsity letters for his track work.

He was always looking to find ways to be a better runner. Part of this included looking to find the best possible shoes for running. This was because he, like many other runners, struggled with shocks on their feet from running so often.

A general desire to lighter shoes was especially important to him. By wearing lighter shoes when running, it would be easier for anyone to move without all that much drag being produced.

After graduating from Oregon, he entered the Army. After a year of active duty, he entered the Stanford Graduate School of Business and earned a master's degree in business administration in 1962.

Discovering His Interest In Shoes

Phil Knight knew that it was important to have good shoes when running. Great shoes help athletes to continue to run at their best possible levels. Shoes are important as they keep people comfortable while running and can keep the feet from suffering from more fatigue than necessary. Being able to get comfortable shoes to work was important to Knight and

While at Stanford, he took a course on business operations. The course was taught by Frank Shallenberger, a professor whose words certainly triggered a substantial response.

Knight had a project in his course that went through the entire semester. The project entailed looking to design a business. This includes the need to design a good marketing campaign for that business.

Knight's belief was that he could order products from Japan that were made with the best quality and the lowest price. This came with the knowledge that the cost of making products was much lower in Japan than it was elsewhere in the United States.

By producing products in Japan and shipping them to the United States, it would be easy for people to find top-quality shoes without having to spend too much to get them.

This concept came about because he knew that it would be easier for people to buy shoes that were comfortable and easy to use without breaking the bank. At the time, the German company Adidas was a very popular brand. This was especially the case with track athletes. However, Adidas and other European countries typically charged more money for their products because the people who made them in Europe were earning more money at their jobs.

In addition, Asia was quickly becoming a continent where skilled industries were becoming more popular. The days of farm labor were dying off as the industrial sector in Asia became more factory-based with an emphasis on teaching people how to complete manufacturing jobs that could benefit not only Asia but the rest of the world.

Knight proposed this concept to Shallenberger. While Shallenberger felt that the concept was interesting, he did not find it to be too viable at the moment. It was still an intriguing concept in spite of his belief that it would be too difficult to make this work.

Those words impacted Knight as he knew that there had to be a way to make this business strategy work. He knew that by getting in touch with Asian companies, it would be easier for a business to thrive and be profitable. After all, many of these Asian companies could certainly become more popular if it started to target people outside of that continent. Still, the need to find a way to make it work was a concern that had to be met in some way.

The process of selling shoes was a pipe dream for the most part at the time. It wasn't until a trip to Kobe, Japan in late 1962 when he had a sudden revelation.

Knight was on a world tour not long after graduating from Stanford. He discovered the Tiger brand of running shoes from the Onitsuka Company in Kobe. He was surprised at how well-made the shoes were even as they were light in weight and could still absorb shocks well. The fact that these shoes were low in cost especially impressed him.

This led to Knight having a meeting with the head of the Onitsuka Company. Knight talked with the company about finding a way to get these shoes to be sold in the western United States.

The biggest thing that Knight wanted to do was to sell these shoes to people around Oregon. He felt that these shoes were very impressive and that it would be rather easy for anyone to run well while wearing them. With this in mind, he felt that it would be easy to sell these shoes to more people all around.

It took a year for Knight to get his first shipment of Tiger shoes out to Oregon but after he got them, he sent a few pairs to Bill Bowerman. He was the head track and field coach at the University of Oregon.

Knight's Great Partner

While Phil Knight was very efficient in terms of getting his products out here to more people, he knew that he could not do it alone. He got help from his old track and field coach to help him with getting the shoes to become more popular.

Bill Bowerman was a prominent track and field coach who spent 25 years coaching Oregon's track athletes. He also trained a number of athletes for the 1968 Summer Olympics and became a head coach for various athletes at the 1972 games.

Bowerman's Oregon runners included more than thirty Olympians and more than sixty All-Americans. Phil Knight was among the many runners that Bowerman coached.

Bowerman had always been interested in finding great shoes that were light in weight and could still resist shocks. This led to Knight getting in touch with him about Tiger shoes and how well they can work. Knight contacted Bowerman in 1963 about the Tiger shoes. This was in the hopes that Bowerman would approve of them and help him out with selling them. It turned out that Bowerman really liked the shoes that Knight gave him. He agreed to be a partner with Knight in his business endeavor and would also supply him with future designs.

In early 1964, the two agreed to a partnership and formed Blue Ribbon Sports. The two invested $500 each in the company to start running the company. They continued to work with Onitsaka to continue to make and sell shoes for the western United States. The business would especially focus on track athletes. Knight and Bowerman would use their experience in the track industry to highlight their shoes and add a sense of credibility to the products that they were selling.

It was at this point that the foundation of Nike was first laid. It would only become a more powerful and influential business as time went along.

Chapter 2 – Growing Nike

Blue Ribbon Sports proved to be a rather popular entity but it wasn't easy for it to grow at the start. Knight wasn't able to make this his only endeavor. During the first few years of operation, Knight supplemented his income by working as a certified public accountant. He also taught some courses at Portland State University.

During his time away from the school and his accounting work, he would drive out to different track meets all around Oregon and other spots in the Pacific Northwest. He drove a green Plymouth Valiant car to these events and would sell those shoes to people all around the area.

He chose these track meets because he knew these were the best places for him to sell his shoes at. After all, he knew that athletes would want to find only the best shoes for the job at hand. Considering how the shoes he was selling weren't available anywhere else, he knew that it would be easy for him to sell his shoes to people who really needed them.

Still, Knight carried through with the intention of making his work more visible. He knew that it was up to his reputation as a track and field star and his overall background in the field to help him sell shoes.

In 1964, the first full year of operation, the company made about $8,000 as about 1,300 pairs of shoes were sold. That total went up to $20,000 in 1965. This helped Blue Ribbon to grow over time to the point where it would be easier for the company to succeed.

The company continued to grow as Knight went out to more track meets around the country. This was effective as more track athletes were supportive of the company as word got out about the shoes that it had to offer. Still, there was a real need to try and make the products more accessible.

While selling shoes from the back of a Valiant was a great way to make money and to get the word out, this was obviously not the most professional way to sell shoes. Knight needed to get more people to pay attention to what he had to offer. Therefore, he had to find a way to get a physical brick and mortar store set up.

Opening Retail Stores

While going around in a car was tough, Knight knew that he had to sell enough shoes to make his business venture worthwhile. Eventually, it got to the point where he made enough money to open a few physical retail stores.

Two physical Blue Ribbon Sports stores opened up in the 1960s. These were located in Santa Monica, California and in Eugene, Oregon, just outside the University of Oregon campus. He started to hire employees at the time with the intention of helping him get the shoes out to more people. The stores were particularly located in spots where track and field activities were popular, what with there being a built-in target audience for the shoes in those places.

As the business grew in size, Knight no longer had a need to sell shoes from the back of his car. In fact, sales grew to the point where he started selling shoes on the eastern half of the country. He opened a distribution center in Massachusetts.

The shoes were especially promoted as places that offered unique Tiger shoes. These stores were the only places where people could buy these shoes. The partnership that he held in Asia helped him to get more of these shoes out to the public.

It took a while for Knight to get it all to work. The expenses associated with running the business certainly went up but it was all with the intention of making his products more visible to everyone.

It would not be until 1969 when he was able to get out of his accounting and teaching job to sell shoes on a full time basis. In fact, he sold about $1 million in shoes that year.

The effort that Knight put into growing his business certainly took years to handle. However, Knight's persistent helped him out with getting Blue Ribbon to become more prominent. This came as he sold more quality products over time. As more track and field runners bought these shoes, those runners became more interested in the products that were being sold. They also spread the word around about the products that Knight was selling.

The Split

While the partnership that Knight had with Onitsuka was especially strong, there were some disputes between them over how business operations were to run. Although Knight successfully managed to get Onitsuka's Tiger shoes sold quite well, the two sides wanted to move in different directions. This especially came as Knight wanted to make newer shoes and work with different designs. In addition, there were some disputes between the two sides over how contracts between them were to be run.

The disputes prompted the two sides to split off from each other in 1971. Onitsuka went its own separate way and would eventually merge with a few other Japanese companies to become Asics, a popular competitor to Nike.

As for Knight, he and Bill Bowerman both went out to develop their own shoes instead of just sell shoes from Japan. They wanted to create shoes with a very special vision in mind. This entailed more than just making shoes that looked appealing and would stand out from the rest of the pack.

A New Vision

The visions that Knight and Bowerman had involved a good look at the needs that the athlete held. They understood that athletes wanted to find great shoes that not only looked appealing but were also comfortable. This included a need to create enough support for the feet to make the shoe fit well while also keeping shocks from being a huge threat.

The key was to create shoes that the athlete could utilize. This was all about making the athlete more competitive and efficient on the track or in any other place.

The new company's name was also chosen to be symbolic. Jeff Johnson, a long-time employee at the retail stores for Blue Ribbon, came up with the name for the business. He chose the name Nike after the Greek goddess of victory. The decision was symbolic of the desire that people had to succeed.

The daughter of the gods Pallas and Styx, Nike is known for her visible wings. She is symbolic of speed and strength. She is especially associated with the desire to succeed in competition. Jeff Johnson determined that Nike would be the perfect name for the business.

In 1971, the Nike name was used for the first time. In addition, a special logo was created. Portland State University design student Carolyn Davidson was commissioned by Knight to create a logo for Nike. She developed a logo that was symbolic of Nike's wings. It had a smooth curved design that was symbolic of the speed and power that Nike was known for holding. The logo was known as the Swoosh.

The Swoosh continues to be the iconic brand symbol that Nike uses to this day. The Swoosh has become recognized all around the world and today is found on just about every product that Nike sells.

Creating Good Shoe Principles

The principles that Knight and Bowerman had were important to the development of Nike. There was a need to create shoes with many points in mind. First, there was a need to keep the outside part of the shoe looking bright and yet light in weight. The use of lightweight rubber materials was especially important. It allowed for a flexible shape without adding more weight than necessary.

The use of dual-density foam was especially important. The foam was designed for the midsole to be flexible and comfortable while retaining its shape for as long as possible. In addition, the foam was organized around parts of the sole where the foot would be more likely to make a stronger impact on the ground while running. This was used to keep the shocks that were felt while running from being much of a threat.

The heel was an important part of the shoe to consider. The heel had to be raised as a means of keeping the Achilles tendon from being at risk of substantial strains. This especially kept the user comfortable while keeping the risk of irritation from being more of a threat than it had to be.

The principles that were devised were made to make the products that Knight and Bowerman wanted to sell unique. The key was to create the most comfortable shoes around so athletes could continue to perform to their best. They could continue to perform without having to adjust themselves midway through the keep the pains and fatigue that came from running from being a threat.

Introducing the Cortez

The Nike Cortez was released in 1972. This was the first official track shoe that Nike had to offer. It was particularly introduced at the Olympic track and field trials in Eugene, Oregon.

The Cortez was designed by Bowerman to create a shoe that would work for distance runners. It was light in weight and features the many design concepts that were devised to create a comfortable and appealing shoe that would keep fatigue from being a threat.

Of course, the Swoosh was also prominent on the shoe. This Swoosh was found around the two sides of the shoe to make it more noticeable.

The Cortez became a very popular shoe among track athletes. They loved how the shoes were rather relaxed and easy to bring out.

This helped make Nike popular but it needed a little bit of extra support to get off the ground. Knight knew that in order to get the business to grow, there was a need to find an athlete who could endorse the product. This was to show that particular athletes could wear particular products and perform well while wearing them. Fortunately, it did not take long for the business to grow and become a bigger overall name.

The First Endorsement

One of the most important points about Nike has come from the many athlete endorsements that the company has acquired. It all started with one legendary and influential runner.

University of Oregon star Steve Prefontaine was the first big star to support Nike's shoes. He became very popular for how he was a dominant and beloved track star in Oregon. He was capable of running a mile in less than four minutes and set the American record in the 5000 meter run during the 1972 Olympic trials.

However, Prefontaine was unable to win a medal at the 1972 Olympics. Still, he won every single NCAA race that he competed in at the 5000 and 10,000 meter and three and six-mile levels. He continued to highlight Nike's shoes over the years and got other track athletes to try out Nike's products.

Steve Prefontaine died in an auto wreck in 1975. However, the impact that he had on Nike was significant as he was the first big name to really get the public to see just what made Nike look strong and effective.

It was amazing to see how well Nike was growing over time. Phil Knight's work became very prominent as he started to become an in-demand name in the world of shoes.

But there was still more for Nike to do to become popular. Knight continued to work with a variety of additional ideas to make his business grow. Part of this included a need to offer more exciting products that could get any athlete to become a bigger star.

Chapter 3 – Changing Products and Growing

A great part of what made Phil Knight a star came from how Nike continued to grow with new innovations. Although it was true that Nike was growing in popularity, he knew that there was a need to keep on expanding.

In the middle part of the 1970s, the company began creating newer sole designs. This came after Bill Bowerman poured some latex into a waffle iron. This led to the inspiration of a new sole that had a waffle-like design that provided enough shock protection while still making the shoes feel comfortable.

This helped to make it easier for the company to make what it had more interesting and useful for athletic use. However, Knight knew that in order to grow, there was a need to make the products being sold more appealing. There were many strategies that were used as a means of making it easier for Nike to grow.

The success that Knight fostered helped Nike to grow throughout the 1970s. This led to Nike becoming a bigger name.

Creating New Shoes

Over time, Nike knew that while the Cortez was a popular shoe, there was a need to design newer shoes with better features. Nike started working on the creation of shoes that could be used for more than just track and field. The company focused on creating shoes that could work with more flexible bodies to help them handle the rigorous movements that come about in tennis, basketball and other sports.

The waffle iron sole design that Bowerman developed was especially important. Knight used this design from Bowerman to help create a better sole design. This over time created a more efficient and comfortable shoe that all people could use when performing all sorts of physical activities. This was especially essential to athletes who wanted to stay on their feet and keep on moving right.

New innovations were often being added to the assortment of products that Nike was introducing. In 1979, one particular inventor hired by Knight to develop new technologies for shoes came up with an impressive feature that continues to be found in Nike shoes to this day.

M. Frank Rudy developed a new technology for the Tailwind shoe called Air. Air technology was designed with plastic membranes filled with gas being added to the soles. The gas was added to create an added cushion while also securing the foot and keeping it relaxed.

Watching Endorsements

Phil Knight focused more on promoting his product by showing people that the product legitimately works. While advertising could help, he felt that there was a real need to show that people can go far when using Nike products. That is, just telling people to buy products or showcasing the features of these products wasn't going to be good enough. Besides, he felt that advertising wasn't always the key to making it easier for products to become visible and attractive and appealing.

The endorsements that Nike had gotten over time were especially critical to the development of the business. Steve Prefontaine's endorsement was particularly important. However, there was a need to get Nike's products to become available for more than just track and field use.

Nike started to make shoes for general sports use. This included shoes that would be used for tennis. In particular, the waffle iron-like sole that the company devised was important to helping get Nike to become a more trustworthy option for shoes.

Nike started to sell more shoes for tennis players among other sports. The company soon got an endorsement from tennis star Ille Nastase.

Additional athletes started to endorse the shoes that Nike had been making. If anything, this move was true to the belief that Knight had in how he doesn't feel that advertising is going to truly make everything work out right.

Knight believed that the best way to market or advertise products was to show to the world that they work and that people can indeed be successful if they used these products. This was especially the case with the endorsements that Knight's products earned.

Jimmy Connors, another big name tennis star, particularly made Nike more popular over time. He won a number of major tennis tournaments while wearing Nike shoes.

Fellow tennis star John McEnroe also started wearing Nike shoes. He wore a three-quarter Nike shoe model not long after having ankle issues. He strained a few ankle ligaments and needed a shoe that could offer more control over his ankles. With this in mind, he started wearing the three-quarter shoes that Nike had been offering at the time. This helped him to keep his ankles steady while having a much easier time moving along the court.

Nike was truly growing in popularity as the company started to offer more products for sale and was especially productive in terms of what was being offered. However, there were some real concerns held by the people at Nike in terms of what they were offering and how competition was starting to come about.

Chapter 4 – Simple Struggles and How They Were Fixed

Although Nike was certainly growing in popularity with new shoes and technologies coming about, there were a few substantial issues that came in the way of how the business was being run. This kept Nike from being far too strong at first but over time the company was able to rise above these issues. Fortunately, many of these issues were resolved over time. The efforts that Phil Knight used in order to succeed and grow over time were especially important to keeping these problems from being too strong or significant.

Endorsement Charges

Getting plenty of athletes to endorse Nike products was a great deal on the company's end. However, there was a bit of concern in that many of the athletes who had endorsed Nike wanted to be paid for their endorsements. This came as these athletes had been bound in a way to use these products in particular. Nike started to spend millions of dollars each year to get its endorsers to be properly compensated. This kept the business from being able to get too much of a profit.

However, this also placed a strong belief in Phil Knight over how advertising is not necessarily something that has to be emphasized. He felt that advertising was an expensive and difficult process that many people who would be targeted would often ignore. This was especially evidenced in when he made a pitch to get an endorsement from Michael Jordan, a basketball star from the University of North Carolina that was about to get into the professional ranks in the early 1980s. Of course, that partnership with Jordan, as you will read soon, would change everything.

Still, the company had to look carefully in terms of how it was getting in touch with more athletes. This included a need to see that it could be carefully organized properly enough in terms of how much was being spent on endorsements and who was endorsing these products.

The decision to choose Michael Jordan clearly was an influential option that made a difference in terms of how Nike was highlighting itself. However, it required plenty of effort to try and find someone suitable for particular marketing needs.

Trying To Reach Women

Although Nike had experienced a great amount of success with men in terms of the shoes that were being sold, there was a significant concern over how Knight and the rest of the company were trying to promote its products to women.

The board members at Nike did not see much of a need for an aerobics shoe for women to wear. It was as though Nike had been focusing on shoes for men above all else while ignoring the fact that women were starting to take a strong interest in athletic shoes.

As a result of Nike's lack of products for women, other companies started to take the lead and target them. This was especially the case for Reebok, another athletic wear company that had started up not too long ago. Reebok started to make aerobic shoes and other footwear products for women around the late 1970s. This led to Nike struggling to compete with the British company in terms of the women's shoe industry.

Nike had started to make shoes for women as a means of getting them into the fray. The goal was to create good shoes that were efficient for workouts without being too complicated or hard to use. However, the damage to Nike was already done in that women were not necessarily choosing the company.

As it will be profiled a little later on in this book, Nike did put in an effort to brand itself to get women to take the business seriously. This was to allow the business to be more trustworthy among this important crowd.

The Struggle With Creativity

There were also concerns over how creative Nike was. While Nike had become more profitable in in the early 1980s, there were still issues over how well the company was trying to build upon itself.

Nike had an initial public offering with 2.37 million shares of stock available in 1980. Nike continues to be traded on the New York Stock Exchange to this day under the NKE symbol.

However, there were worries over how creative Nike's products were. This came as Nike had not come across any new forms of technology or any radical designs in a while.

This led to Phil Knight coming up with an idea to find a way to market the company around a new name. This led to his meeting with Michael Jordan in 1984.

As Knight established a partnership with Jordan, the goal was to create a brand new shoe that would help his business become even more powerful. This led to the creation of a shoe that would forever change the sport of basketball.

Chapter 5 – The Air Jordan

While Nike had struggled with sales in the early 1980s and tried to make profits in spite of things like costly endorsements or added competition, the company knew that it had to make some changes. This led to Phil Knight making one of the most important decisions in the company's history.

In 1984, Phil Knight met with Michael Jordan, a star college basketball player who played at North Carolina and had been recently drafted by the Chicago Bulls. He was impressed with Jordan's skills and felt that Jordan would become a big star in the NBA. With this in mind, he felt that the best thing the company could do would be to introduce a new shoe based around this big star.

The key was to find someone who was willing to support Nike products and was not as big of a name as others at the time, thus making it easier for the company to afford the endorsement. By sticking with one particular person and doing enough research on that person, it was easy for Nike to make a decision on whom the next big name for the company would be. In this case, it ended up being Michael Jordan, a man who would soon revolutionize the sport of basketball forever.

In 1984, the company released the Michael Jordan 1. This was a shoe that would eventually be renamed the Air Jordan.

Peter C. Moore, an employee for Nike, designed this shoe to feature a red and black paint job to match up with the Bulls' team colors. The Swoosh was still visible on the sides while an extensive white trim could be seen near the bottom part of the shoe.

At first NBA Commissioner David Stern tried to ban the shoe as it did not have all that much white on them. In fact, Stern even issued Jordan a $5,000 fine every time he would play a game with those shoes. This was due to how the shoes did not have the same white color that other shoes had.

However, this provided an amazing marketing opportunity for Nike. While it is true that the Air Jordan 1 was a very efficient shoe and provided enough comfort and support for the feet, Nike marketed it as stating that it could give the player an unfair advantage. This was especially thanks to the knowledge that Jordan was being fined every time he wore those shoes on the court.

The outlaw nature of the Air Jordan was an especially popular point. This was made to make it more outstanding and interesting among people who wanted something unique and different.

The Air Jordan helped get Nike to grow even further. In 1986, Nike got to $1 billion in annual revenue for the first time ever.

An Extended Relationship

Of course, the success of the Air Jordan was something that helped make Phil Knight an even more powerful name in the world of shoes. Over the years, the Air Jordan would be updated with new looks and features. Also, while many Nike shoes were made in Asia, the second edition of the Air Jordan and other versions in the future were made in Italy. This was done as a means of placing an emphasis on luxury materials used in the making of the shoe.

Nike even managed to keep Jordan on board even when he thought about leaving after the second Air Jordan was made. In 1988, Nike employee Tinker Hatfield designed the Air Jordan III. This offered a visible air feature on the heel to add more support and to make the shoe more distinguishable. The Jumpman logo, the famed silhouette of Jordan looking like he is about to slam dunk a ball, was introduced on this shoe too.

Over the years, Nike continued to make the Air Jordan a big hit. Hatfield continued to design a few new editions of the shoe. Filmmaker Spike Lee also promoted the shoe in advertisements with Nike and even had the Air Jordan featured prominent in his influential 1989 film Do the Right Thing.

The Air Jordan continued to be a big name shoe that continued to grow in popularity while Michael Jordan's iconic career continued to blossom. Many special editions of the shoe have been made over the years. Nike even had a promotional campaign with many characters from the Warner Brothers' Looney Tunes cartoon series.

The work that Phil Knight and company made was critical to the success of Nike's success. Even with this, he knew that he had to continue working on the momentum that Nike had gotten in recent time.

Chapter 6 – Moving Forward

Phil Knight had finally gotten his business to take off. Nike was on firm ground as the company had plenty of support in the form of great shoe designs, prominent athletes wearing the company's products and plenty of new shoes for many people.

The company began to make more shoes for women and started to expand to where more sports could benefit from Nike shoes. However, Knight knew that Nike still needed to come up with new things to make the company grow even further.

The Nike Air Max

The Nike Air Max shoe was an important innovation in Nike's history. Introduced in 1987, this offered a larger air cushioning segment. That segment was also visible on the middle part of the shoe. This was used to create a more comfortable and flexible shoe. Knight knew that this shoe was a big deal as it was a revolution in the world of shoes. As a result, he got the company to make a massive splash by becoming the first company to use an original song from the legendary rock back the Beatles in its commercials. The commercials for the Air Max featured the Beatles' Revolution as the shoe's anthem. This remains the only time in history that an original Beatles recording has been used in a television advertisement.

The Air Max became a highly respected shoe among many athletes. This came as people were looking for shoes that were effective enough for their workout needs.

A Special Slogan

While advertising and endorsements were big, Knight knew that in order to make Nike stand out, there had to be a simple slogan that would make the company stick out. That is, it had to be something that was easy to remember and didn't have to be promoted too often.

With this in mind, advertising mogul Dan Wieden devised a slogan that was made with the intention of being very intense and personal – "Just do it."

While Reebok was focused on easy-going athletics, Nike devised the Just Do It campaign as a more aggressive counterpart. It was used to target athletes who wanted to give their all out on the court, track or anywhere else they were.

This was especially designed to resolve the issue of Nike not targeting women. In particular, it was designed as a more universal slogan for all people regardless of age or gender or background to follow. It suggested that no matter what one wants to get out of physical activities, the best thing a person can do is to stop thinking about something and to just do it.

This slogan helped Nike to grow in popularity. More customers started to consider Nike products over time, thus leading to added revenues and sales.

Of course, Nike continued to use many other advertising campaigns. The company made one campaign with two-sport athlete Bo Jackson known as "Bo Knows." They also made a series of advertisements with Charles Barkley were the basketball star was more personal about his views on why people shouldn't idolize athletes.

The advertisements were successful in that they focused more on the attitude of Nike and how important the right products can be to one's success. This was also to emphasize how Nike is a brand that targets those who are more committed to success. The most important part of the advertisements is that Nike wanted to show that while appearance can make a difference, performance is what really matters. Those who can actually perform to the best standards that they hold were the ones that could succeed and do anything in the sports world.

Keep an Ethical Image

Although Nike was indeed growing in popularity, there were worries about how Asian manufacturers responsible for making Nike products were treated. This led Knight to make some dramatic changes in terms of how Nike products were to be made.

Knight was long inspired by many practices that Asian businesses had in terms of doing business and making products. However, there were concerns over how the conditions at Asian manufacturing plants had become extremely difficult. Part of this included problems relating to extreme working hours, child labor and a general sense of neglect over the welfare of the people who were making products. The fact that many of these people were not paid all that much money certainly hurt even more.

This led to Knight making the decision to change how the manufacturing standards within Nike were to be followed. In particular, new programs were established to ensure that Nike products were made in a safer and more supportive environment.

For instance, the minimum working age was increased by a few years. Also, more non-toxic materials were being used in the factories making shoes. These included safer and easier to handle glues that did not produce potentially harmful fumes.

Air quality standards were also improved within their factories in Asia. These include standards that meet American requirements relating to keeping the air clear and healthy so all people in the workplace could breathe easy. Also, new education programs were established at these factories to improve the efficiency of employees and to make it easier for them to produce products in less time, thus keeping them from having to work longer than necessary.

Expanding Its Reach

One other point that Knight wanted to do was to expand Nike's reach to include more sports. This led to Nike developing new brands relating to soccer, golf and many other sports.

As Nike developed more products, it led to more endorsements from a variety of popular athletes and teams. The Brazilian national soccer team scored a substantial endorsement deal with Nike, for instance. In 1996, the company signed Tiger Woods to an endorsement deal. This came as the golfing prospect left his amateur status to compete as a professional. Like with Michael Jordan in basketball before him, Tiger Woods would end up revolutionizing golf.

Nike also started to sell more athletic apparel including shorts and tops for athletes to wear. These included plenty of products designed to be light in weight while also resisting moisture.

The company even got into the field of making artificial turf materials. Old shoes that were not being used after wear were recycled and made into different synthetic flooring surfaces. This came through the Nike Grind system. The system helped to product a variety of carpet underlays, indoor synthetic surfaces, running tracks and artificial turf infill materials. These were designed to create the best playing or running surfaces possible.

Indeed, Nike had it all in terms of shoes. However, Nike continued to grow and keep on thriving as a means of showing the world that it was more than just a pretty brand.

Chapter 7 – Recent Developments

In 1999, Nike co-founder Bill Bowerman died at 88 years of age. This was a big turning point in Nike's history as it left Phil Knight on his own to continue running the company.

This was an important time but Knight knew that he had to keep on getting the company to work well enough and to stay influential. Part of this included working hard to get Nike to become a more profitable entity.

Knight felt that while being on top of the world was important, it is even more important to get the public to see that a company still has new ideas. That is, it is essential to keep on proving to the world that one still has strong concepts.

In 2000, Nike introduced a brand new technology for its shoes. This was called Nike Shox, a performance feature that continues to be highlighted to this day. Shox works with a few hollow columns located around the midsoles. These were made of rubber. Shox were designed to look like protrusions on the end of the shoe. These are capable of absorbing a variety of shocks that one experiences while walking. They could also spring back and bring about more power onto the foot's movement. The elastic properties of the Shox features especially made the product more efficient and easy for people to wear on a variety of surfaces.

The product became very popular throughout the 2000s as more basketball stars began to wear them and ask for them. The shoes were even popular among those outside the athletic realm as many people looked for Shox shoes to find options that could keep their feet comfortable even during a long day of work. Celebrities like Hugh Laurie and Jerry Seinfeld were particularly fond of these shoes. Laurie even said that he had a few dozen pairs of Shox shoes that he wore while working on the set of his hit television series House.

Nike especially continued to grow in size as in 2003 the company spent a little more than $300 million to acquire Converse. Knight made the decision to acquire Converse as that company had been trying to recover from a bankruptcy. The fact that 1980s trends were coming back around that time was important. Many of Converse's shoes, particularly its iconic Chuck Taylor high-tops, were expected to become big again. With this in mind, Nike bought Converse and retained the Converse brand to highlight new models and designs of these popular street shoes. Of course, Chuck Taylor shoes were still the most popular items that Converse had to offer. Nike went as far as to add its own technology to those shoes. Today a new edition of the Chuck Taylor All-Star shoe has a lighter insole and a more flexible body while still retaining the classic appearance that it has sported for generations.

His Work Outside Nike

While Phil Knight continued to be a prominent name in the world of shoes and athletic goods, he continued to do more outside of Nike. In 2006, he made a donation of $105 million to the Stanford Graduate School of Business. This was the largest individual donation to a business school at the time. Meanwhile, Knight has donated millions of dollars to the University of Oregon. He funded a multi-million dollar football facility and helped support the production of many scholarship programs at the school. He even helped with the funding process for the construction of a new basketball arena.

Nike also helped with funding much of the cost associated with producing uniforms for many of the school's teams. The company has particularly made the school famous for how it has an assorted variety of uniform combinations for its football team. In particular, there are thousands of different possible football uniform combinations for the Ducks to wear based on colors and other features that may be added.

In 2008, Knight donated $100 million to the Oregon Health and Science University Cancer Institute. The Portland-based school has worked to promote cancer research in the hopes of finding a cure in the future.

Knight even got into the film industry as he put in a stake in a film production company. In 1998, Knight purchased a stake in a studio run by production mogul Will Vinton. Knight even purchased Will Vinton Studios and eventually rebranded the company Laika. The company continues to make films to this day.

The End

The amazing thing about Phil Knight's work is that he continued to keep on working to make a difference even as his days at Nike were coming to an end. In 2015, he retired as the chairman of Nike. He owned close to 65 million shares of stock in the company. Today Nike CEO and president Mike Parker is the main chairman of the company. Parker has particularly been heralded for focusing on sustainable business practices and engineering green products.

As of 2015, Phil Knight's net worth was about $28 billion. Forbes' Billionaires List has him rated as the 24th wealthiest person in the world, just ahead of Microsoft's Steve Ballmer and Forrest, Jacqueline and John Mars of the Mars candy company family.

Nike continues to be a prominent name in shoes to this day. Nike has more than 60,000 employees all over the world and sells its shoes in stores all over. The company makes about $30 billion in revenue every year and gets a general profit of about $3 billion each year.

Conclusion – What You Can Learn From Phil Knight

So, what can you learn from the story of Phil Knight and how he got Nike to become one of the world's most successful shoe companies? There are a few important lessons that his story can teach you about how important hard work and the ability to create new ideas can make a difference.

Unique Ideas

First, you can certainly learn from the work that Knight made that it takes a unique business plan to make it easier for anyone to succeed. Knight had the idea of getting in touch with companies and factories in Japan to make affordable and top-quality products for people to buy. This was a unique concern at the time as not many people thought about contacting Asian companies for products.

Having a unique idea can make a real difference when it comes to growing a business. Phil Knight had such a great idea and this helped his business venture to become successful.

Being able to convey his ideas to people was important. While he might not have gotten as much support from his instructor as he wished, he knew that it was up to him to get the word out. The eventual meeting that he had with an Asian business about selling shoes in the United States proved to be the key to his success in getting people to take what he was offering seriously.

Effort

Second, it takes effort to make it in any business world. Knight knew that he had to put in plenty of work to make his products more visible and popular. Part of this included a need to go out there to as many events as possible to promote Nike shoes at the start.

Back during the Blue Ribbon days, Knight knew that he had to get out there to more track meets to promote the shoes that he got from Japan. It was the only way how he could market himself as he needed to show that he was serious about getting track athletes to perform to their best abilities.

A Drive To Move Forward

Getting a business off of the ground and making it successful is a tall order for anyone. Phil Knight was able to get Nike off the ground and to make it stand out. However, he knew that just getting Nike to grow and thrive was not good enough.

The need to create new products and innovations was critical. Over the years, Nike expanded to offer more products for a variety of athletes. The many innovations that Nike came across over the years certainly made its products unique.

Of course, the various endorsements from high-level athletes certainly helped Nike to keep on growing. However, none of this would have worked without the effort that Knight and the rest of the people at Nike had put in to keep moving forward even when they were already at the top.

If anything, the Just Do It slogan that Nike has lived by over the years is symbolic of the company in general. Nike started out as a small business but by having a desire to get out there and perform with no worries, the company managed to grow and become a huge success story. If anything, Nike is a business that truly lives by the motto that it created.

Today you can learn quite a bit from what Phil Knight did when building his shoe empire. The work that Knight made to get to where he is today certainly helped him to become a stronger person in today's fitness and fashion world.

Remember, the next time you see a pair of Nike shoes or someone wearing something with that distinguishable Swoosh logo, think about the effort that went into making that product. You'll remember that it all came about as Phil Knight worked his hardest to grow Nike and to make it all stand out. It's truly amazing as to how this all came out at the start out of the back of a green Plymouth Valiant.

Printed in Great Britain
by Amazon

28433870R00030